# Turn Your Home Into a Rental House Instead of Selling it!

## Terry Sprouse
## Angy Sprouse

Planeta Books LLC
Tucson, Arizona

ISBN 978-0-9798566-5-5

Published by: Planeta Books LLC
*www.fixemuprentemout.com*

# Acknowledgements

We thank the amazing Randy Cramer for his editing and insightful comments in reviewing this book.

# Turn Your Home Into a Rental House Instead of Selling It!

# Table of Contents

Turn Your Home Into a Rental House Instead of Selling It!

# Introduction

## Don't set your sights too low

*The greatest danger for most of us is not that our aim is too high and we miss it, but that it is too low and we reach it.*
-- Michelangelo

According to the *American Association of Realtors*, the average American purchases seven houses during their lifetime. In our opinion, those are seven houses that you should hold onto for the rest of our lives. They are valuable assets that will generate monthly income for the hard years to come, and provide further assurance of long-term economic family security. Like the old folktale says: "Don't kill the goose that lays the golden eggs."

The common path most people follow to achieve their American Dream is to sell the home that they currently live in, then use the cash from the sale to buy a new house. This is the standard template proven many times over to be a system that works. But a little tweaking of this old but worn road to security can convert your home into something more profitable. Wouldn't we all like to get the best from our home investment? Wouldn't we all prefer an increase in our net worth and further fortify our economic security? Wouldn't we all like to have our own island and like Marlon Brando, be so well off that we don't even need to show up for our own Oscar?

Anyway, here is what we propose. Instead of selling your home, just refinance it, and use the money from the refinance as a down payment on your next house. Now, you own two houses. One is your home for you and your family. And the second home is working for you, the contented owner of a profitable rental property.

To get there follow these three easy steps:

Step Number 1. Refinance your residence.

Step Number 2. Use the refinance money as a down payment to buy a new house.

Step Number 3. Move into the new house and rent out the old house.

It is as simple as that.

When is the best time to make this significant decision?

The time to maximize the steps shown above is when you realize that your existing house no longer meets the needs of your family. Perhaps you bought a house as a young couple and now that you have children the house suddenly seems too small. Maybe your job requires you to relocate, or you just don't like the neighborhood anymore. There are many other reasons that may come to your mind that arise from your own situation. Nonetheless, for one reason or another, you find that you need to make change, but you are not sure which way to turn. So let's look at some of the pros and cons of these three simple steps.

## Advantages to owning two houses

Two immediate advantages to owning two houses instead of one that come to mind are:

1.) New and additional source of income. You have a your cash flow in the form of rental checks regularly received on a monthly basis, all coming from your old house. This income provides a new layer of security that does not depend on you investing regular hours like "Workin' 9 to 5, what a way to make a livin'," (Dolly Parton 1980).'

Furthermore, the cash continues to flow even when you, "...get the nerve to say, take this job and shove it," (Johnny Paycheck 1999), and you lose your normal job. While you may not be fans of the "music" mentioned above, or ever agree that it is music, we think you must agree that an additional source of income is always welcomed.

2.) Your equity accelerates like a race car. Equity is the difference between how much the home is worth and how much you owe on the mortgage. Formerly, you had only one house that was increasing in value an average of 5% each year, now you have two houses, both going up in value.

For example, a $200,000 house would increase in value to $300,000 over 10 years. That's $100,000 in equity that you make just from owning just that one piece of property. When you own two houses your equity would increase to $200,000 in ten years.

There are also several tax advantages to owning rental property worth mentioning: tax deductions for depreciation, for repairs, and for travel. Our government wants us to succeed in our real estate business. That's why they gave us all the tax breaks.

Our elected officials can be egotistical and self-serving. Washington DC is the only place where you can see a prominent congressman walking down Lover's Lane holding his own hand. Still, despite their faults, they occasionally

11

manage to do things that actually help us.

Another thing to keep in mind, when you are a real estate investor, you make your money by relying on long term trends. We have all experienced the volatile times when house values actually go down in the short term, like when the country's economy is in a recession.

Yet, in the long-term, despite fits and starts in the economy, home values still show the trend of going up. According the *U.S. Census Bureau*, from 1940 to 2010, the average increase in the value of a house was about 5% per year, adjusted for inflation (U.S. Census Bureau, 2012). This is important because home and rental investments should be viewed as something that will be with us for the rest of our lives.

## Disadvantages and how to address them

Along with the upsides to owning rental properties, of course there are also some important and demanding issues to consider. Here are some we like to look at as small and manageable issues rather than big obstacles.

- There is work required to prepare your house to rent out;
- Time must be spent finding and managing tenants;
- Life is fraught with problems. Even tenants have a few.

But listen to this. The financial reward is worth the time spent to learn how to successfully manage these issues.

We will discuss how to address these concerns in Chapters 2 through 5.

## Let's see what the future looks like

If you get out your crystal ball, one that gives you a look into the future (we got ours an eBay), and light your spiritually inspiring incense, you will immediately see the results of never selling a home. The future reflected from the glittering ball is one where all your purchased homes are turned into rental properties.

You feel the satisfaction of knowing that as a result of your diligence over the years, you now have accumulated six or seven rental houses. You have benefited from years of monthly checks from your tenants. You have achieved enlightenment (maybe) and the American Dream (more likely). Or at least, enough for you to enjoy a comfortable and worry free retirement.

In this future, your houses continue to provide you with a substantial flow of monthly income, which in many ways is like an additional pension. Only later, you may decide to sell one of your properties, retrieve the funds for an investment for your children or needy relatives, or to splurge on that vacation you've always dreamed of. Go ahead, you earned it. You've paid your dues. Owning a stable of seven houses presents you with many options that you might not otherwise have had.

This is what these three steps are intended to provide: a good, strong retirement where you can be healthy and happy, enjoy life and really enjoy your family without the hassles of a heavy financial burden. You might achieve this the old way, selling your home, then buying another, but here we will show you that keeping your home is an option that can reap greater benefit.

## Our astonishing story

Now let us tell you a little about us. We (Terry & Angy, remember us?) are partners in both marriage and in real estate business. (Who says married couples can't be business partners? And the great thing is we have never considered divorce . . . murder sometimes, but never divorce. Well, never murder, really, but maybe forcing each other to watch, in an uninterrupted viewing, the horrendously mind numbing *Clan of the Cave Bear.*) In reality, this business has been a bonding experience, not only for us, as husband and wife, but also for our two boys, who have been active participants in the business from the very beginning.

We started in real estate investing following the terrorist attacks on the World Trade Center. The ensuing economic recession forced our hand. The hours at Terry's job were drastically reduced. We realized that for the security of our family, we needed to have a business on the side—a business able to provide regular cash flow in case Terry's 9 to 5 job suddenly went away.

This led Terry to experience a very intensive period of soul searching and in-depth research (accompanied by gratuitous whining and moping). We decided that a rental house business was the best way to go. We were excited to find the rental business was an easy business to learn and to start. This business required no special license, degree, or training. And the results tempered the most important source of Terry's whining. The rental business offered the potential to make money.

We simply started with buying an inexpensive fixer-upper house, one that had foreclosed and been repossessed by a bank. We moved into and lived in the fixer-upper house while we did the necessary repairs. But most important, we did not sell our original home. We rented it out.

It took a little adjustment to move into that first fixer-upper house. The first thing we did was to get one of the bathrooms back into working condition. Angy's negotiating stance on that topic was, "I'm not living in that house unless at least one bathroom is fully operational!" At that, who could argue? Marveled by a mother's logic, together Terry and the boys nodded their heads and dropped the labeled empty plastic bottles they held in their hand into the Recycle Box.

As we went forward with the repairs, we changed bedrooms frequently. Moving from room to room, we cleared out of one bedroom to install tile and then moved again out of the next to make room to install carpet. Huffing and puffing, we moved furniture from one side to the next as we worked through the house painting all the walls. We replaced the cabinets in the kitchen, the fixtures in the bath, the leaky plumbing and the outdated lighting.

Preparing meals required serious creativity. Entertainment and rest required the same. But the support and flexibility from all family members, and a few timely "group hugs" (some through gritted teeth), got us through.

## Like having an additional pension without retiring – only better!

Speaking of pensions, you may find that owning rental houses far exceeds the benefit of the pension that you could receive from your job. Terry worked for the state of Arizona for 13 years, and he will one day receive a pension of around $1,000 a month.

But guess what? Each year the value of Terry's pension will go down because it is not tied to inflation. So, after 10 years we'll still receive $1,000 a month, but because of inflation it may actually be only worth $100 dollars a month as the cost of our groceries, our clothes, health care, and other expenses have all gone up each year.

While we could chose the option of stocking up on essential supplies, there is a limit to the number of peanut butter jars we can stuff into the old storage shed. And what are the squirrels going to think if our hoarding affects their supply of nuts? It could lead to some uncomfortable confrontations in the park when we're out walking the dog.

Rental houses provide a better "pension." If we receive $1,000 a month in rental profits, it not only keeps up with inflation, but it usually exceeds inflation. And, as we mentioned earlier, the same is true for the value of our houses. Which pension program would your rather have? One that increases in value with the passing years, or one that decreases in value?

## Do what millionaires do?

What do millionaires do that most people don't do?
Go into politics?
Buy their own *Starbucks*?
Become a bearded recluse?
Well, those are some of the things they do, but according to Thomas Stanley, in *The Millionaire Next Door*, most American millionaires own their own houses, and they own at least one rental property.

Our perspective is, "if it works for millionaires, it ought to work for us too."

Our fondest hope is that this book will inspire you to buy a rental property and to receive the enormous benefits from that one bold action. Even if you buy just one rental property throughout the course of your entire life, your economic picture will almost immediately get better. You will wonder, as we did, "Why didn't we do this a long time ago?"

In the next chapter, you will learn the critical first step to owning your first rental home.

# Chapter 1
# Refinance Your Home & Buy a New One

The first step in this process is to refinance your present home, and take some cash out of your home equity to use as a down payment to purchase your next home.

Refinancing is similar to the process you encountered when you closed on your first mortgage. It requires an application, credit check, a title search, as well as the usual cost of an appraisal and inspection fees. Actually, the process of refinancing a home is much easier and is completed quicker than when going through the process of buying a home and getting the mortgage.

When we first refinanced our townhouse to get money to purchase another house, we were a little nervous. We thought, "Is this going to create too much a financial burden for us to pay two mortgages at the same time?" But, it turned out that we never had to pay two mortgages at once.

That's because while we were going through the six-week long closing process to purchase our new house, we kept ourselves busy preparing our "old" house to rent out. The same day that we closed on the "new" house and moved in, we put the "For Rent" sign up on our "old" house. One week later, we had tenants renting our "old" house.

The monthly payments of the tenants covered the cost of the mortgage, taxes, insurance, utilities, and the "princely sum" of $40 left over was profit for us. After a few years passed, and we learned to adjust our rental price to what other rental houses were getting in the area, we started clearing around $300 per month. (See Chapter 4 for some perfectly legal ways to increase your rental profits, which don't require drawing a gun or subtly displaying the threatening DVD cover of *Plan 9 from Outer Space*).

The beauty of this process lies in its ease and relative safety. On the other hand, if you were to buy a rental property without using our technique, you might spend a couple months making repairs before you could move some tenants in and begin to have your expenses covered by the rental payment. In that case it could create some economic hardship because you would be paying two mortgages at the same time.

It's like the difference between taking a small jump over a little stream verses taking a giant leap over a wide river. We prefer to keep our shoes dry.

## Cash-out mortgage refinancing

Cash-out mortgage refinancing involves refinancing your mortgage for more than you currently owe and pocketing the difference. If you have been paying down your mortgage for some time, then the principal is likely to be substantially lower than what it was when you first took out your mortgage. That build-up of equity will allow you to take out a loan that covers what you currently owe, and then some.

For example, let's say you buy a house for $200,000. You make a down payment of $20,000 and borrow $180,000. The day you buy the house, your equity is the same as the down payment, $20,000. That's $200,000 (home's purchase price) - $180,000 (amount owed) = $20,000 (equity).

Fast-forward ten years. You have been making your monthly payments faithfully, and have paid down $13,000 of the mortgage debt, so you now owe $167,000. During the same time, the value of the house has increased. Now it is worth $300,000. Your equity is $133,000: $300,000 (home's current appraised value) - $167,000 (amount owed) = $133,000 (equity). See the Table 1.

*Table 1*

*House purchase price $200,000*
*Amount borrowed -180,000*
*Down payment/equity $20,000*


*Ten Years Later*
*Amount borrowed $180,000*
*Principal paid -$23,000*
*Amount owed $167,000*

*House's appraised value $300,000*
*Amount owed -167,000$*
*Equity $133,000*


In this example, you owe $167,000 on the $300,000 house and want $40,000 for a down payment on a new house. You could refinance your mortgage for $207,000, and the bank will then hand over a check to you for the difference of $40,000 ($207,000 - $167,000 = $40,000).

**Put your lazy equity to work**

We all know lazy teenagers who survive on chicken nuggets and sleep all day without engaging in any productive activities other than achieving Level 44 in the latest video game of *Zombies v. Vampires*. These teenagers need to get a job at *McDonalds,* or post himself wearing a purple hoody and singing "Nevah say Nevah!" on *You Tube,* and turn all that excess wasted time into making money.

The same is true of your home equity. It's just lounging around on the beach and drinking margaritas. That lazy equity can be put to work by *you* using *it* to purchase a second house. That is how you get things back under control. You should be the one lounging on the beach and drinking margaritas, not your home equity.

## The refinancing rule

When you refinance your home mortgage to convert some of our equity in your home into cash you should be aware also that your loan balance and monthly payment may be higher than before. The rule to remember is to never pay more for the mortgage than you take in from rent payments.

Let us repeat that. Never pay more for the mortgage than you take in from rent payments. That's a recipe for disaster. Ideally, the rent you charge to the tenants should always cover all the expenses of the mortgage, as well as be enough to provide you with a monthly income.

## Fixed-rate vs. adjustable rate mortgages

There are two basic types of mortgages: those with "fixed" (or, unchanging) interest rates and those with adjustable (or variable) rates (ARMs). ARMs can change after a predetermined amount of time has passed, such as one year or five years. While an adjustable-rate mortgage (ARM) will try to entice us by offering a lower introductory rate than a fixed-rate mortgage, the ARM's rate could dramatically jump in the future if interest rates rise.

As investors, we need to know how much we pay for our mortgage each month, with no surprises. ARMs are particularly dangerous when mortgage interest rates are low, because they have no way to go but up. It makes much more sense to opt for the predictability and security of a fixed rate loan.

This is like when we go to the 21 screen multiplex cinemas. Should we buy tickets to the reliable *Saw IX*? Or take a risk at spending the $22.50 per person ticket price, including popcorn and large drink, for the more unpredictable, likely phoned in, Nicholas Cage performance? (Angy comment: "I'd rather be watching *Midnight in Paris*.")

## An added benefit to refinancing

Refinancing a loan differs from purchasing a house in that you can roll the closing costs into the loan.

That means that if you take out a $100,000 loan, and closing costs are 3%, or $3,000 dollars, your loan amount changes to $103,000 and you pay the entire amount over the 30 period of the loan. This is a big advantage because you can do the refinancing without any money coming out of your pocket, and you only pay a few extra dollars every month for your loan.

## Shop for a loan

It's important that you shop around and compare costs and terms when you want to refinance your loan. It's also a good idea to know your credit score before you refinance. Costs and terms can vary from lender to lender, so it's wise to compare multiple options. Knowing your credit score gives you the upper hand when lender's cost and terms are based on your credit history.

One of the easiest ways to shop for a loan is through internet lenders like *www.LendingTree.com* or *www.MortgageLoan.com*. These online lenders help match your loan request with several lenders at once and provide you with customized loan offers. You can also confirm the value of the property that you would like to purchase at *www.Eppraisal.com* or *www.zillow.com*.

Then to further harden your search, you may want to inquire about loan offers from local lenders, banks, or credit unions. You may have heard that each time someone runs a credit check on you it lowers your credit score, but the truth is it's likely only lowered by a very small amount.

We have gotten loans both from online companies and from brick-and-mortar companies that have offices in our town. Some people may not feel comfortable getting a mortgage online, but companies, like the ones we mentioned, do not loan money, they just give you a list of loan companies, so that you can compare rates and terms. As long as you work with an established, reputable company you shouldn't have any trouble.

If you wish to check up on a company you can review their *Better Business Bureau* rating at *http://www.bbb.org*. Whichever way you go, it is still important to get multiple offers, because that is the only way to get the best interest rate and lowest overall fees.

On our first house purchase, we were green as a gourd. We made arrangements with a mortgage broker we knew could provide us with the loan. The realtor, who was selling the house, saw that we were getting charged a lot more than necessary for the loan, so he made a friendly suggestion that we get a quote from a second company.

We followed this advice and we were shocked to see that we got a much better interest rate with extremely lower fees from the second company. It was like the difference in cost between a can of *Chicken-of-the-Sea* and an order of *Emeril's Grilled Tuna Steak*. From then on, we always got at least two bids on each new purchase or home refinance that we did.

## Make good use of Good Faith Estimates

When you ask a lender for interest rates and costs for a loan, the lender will get back to you with a "good-faith estimate" (GFE), which details the anticipated costs you can expect to pay for a loan from that company. The costs listed on the GFE typically include the lender's origination fee, points (if any), escrow or attorney's closing fees, title insurance, appraisal fee, and various other taxes and expenses.

Do what we do, and request a good faith estimate (GFE) from various lenders and then select the best one. That reminds us of the nun who practiced exercising good faith.

*A nun who served as a nurse at a St. Joseph's Hospital was in such a rush to work she neglected to refill her car with gas. She ran out of gas about half way to work and was forced to walk to the nearest service station.*

*The service station attendant explained that his gas can was loaned out, so the nun returned to her car in search of anything she could use to carry some gas.*

*She found a hospital bed pan in her trunk, so she went to purchase a gallon of gas. As she was emptied the contents of the bedpan into her car, a truck with two men in it passed by.*

*"Now that's what I call faith!" one said to the other.*

## Purchasing your new home

As mentioned, to purchase your new home, you will use the cash you received from refinancing your old home, as the down payment for a new loan on your next house.

What we recommend is to buy a less expensive fixer-upper house that needs some repair. We try to buy houses in "transition zones," which are locations that are in transition because new types of people and businesses are moving in. We like these areas because we can pay significantly less money to purchase an investment property there. (More on transition zones in Chapter 6.)

If you want to accelerate your accumulation of rental houses, you can move more frequently than just every time you need a new house. Instead, you can move every time you find another good home that meets your requirements (an inexpensive fixer upper house in one of your target areas).

In Chapter 2, we will show you how to get your house ready to rent and how to attract potential tenants to your house, like paparazzi to a red carpet.

## Chapter 2
## Get Your Old House Ready to Rent

Now you have refinanced your home, and you wisely used the money that you received at closing as a down payment on another house that you will soon move to as your new home. It's time to get to work! Here are steps for you to follow to ready your old property for renting out, and steps to find good tenants.

**5 steps to get your house ready to rent**

### Step 1: Remove furniture

Move all of your furniture and personal belongings out of your old house. The absence of these items makes the house look bigger and the home is more inviting if it is not cluttered up with beds, chairs, food supplies, and toys. It also makes it easier to do a thorough job of cleaning the house.

This only applies to the first time you rent out your new rental house. After tenants leave in the future, they will take most of their things with them. Of course, some tenants do not follow the normal procedure, and they may leave in the middle of the night to avoid paying their last rent check.

Occasions like this makes it tempting to slip a magnetized GPS tracking device under the fender of the tenant's car.

An incident like this happened to us a couple of years ago. Not only did the tenant leave a pile of clothing, bottles and boxes of cleaning supplies, cupboards of food, and a sofa, but also left behind a car that didn't work. (So much for the GPS idea.) Most of the things we took to Goodwill, but we kept a few things, like a car battery charger and some paint.

Tenants like this one are the exception. Tenants normally take most of their things with them when they leave; making it easy for us to prepare the property for the next tenant, and without much effort, to present an appealing yet empty house.

### Step 2: A meticulous clean up

Thoroughly clean the house. This includes painting walls (a fresh coat of paint makes the place look and smell good), washing floors, cleaning appliances (especially the oven), shampooing carpets, washing the windows, cleaning the bathrooms and checking the roof.

We always buy a one year's supply of air conditioner/furnace filters for the property. A dirty filter can shorten the life of an air conditioner. Some tenants forget to change the filters, so we send postcards in June with a friendly reminder to change them. As we discuss in Chapter 4, all your interaction with tenants should be in a friendly and professional manner.

### Step 3: If it's broken, repair it

Take care of all repair work before tenants move in. Leave nothing to chance. Change broken outlets and switches, patch holes, remove stains, replace cracked and broken glass, repair dripping faucets, replace missing shingles, and fix roof leaks.

The old saying that "Left to themselves, things always go from bad to worse," is especially true with rental houses. It's tempting to assume that that small leak in the bathtub, or a toilet that flushes most of the time, won't bother anyone.

But trust us, you will invariably get that call to repair the bathtub or toilet at the most inopportune time.

This doesn't mean that everything in the house has to be new, but everything should be in working order. It is a rental house after all, and not *Buckingham Palace.*

For example, bedroom doors do not have to be replaced every time they have a crack or a hole in them. They can be rehabilitated with wood putty and a fresh coat of paint. But, the doors do have to open and close.

The key is that everything in the house works, not that it looks brand new.

## Buy used construction materials

Missing or broken light switches, outlets, covers can be replaced inexpensively with quality used ones. We have also purchased reliable refrigerators, dishwashers, and toilets at stores that recycle construction materials, for pennies on the dollar. The *Habitat for Humanity Store* is one such place that we frequent for good used materials. There are 825 Habitat Stores in the United States and Canada. You can locate a store near you at www.habitat.org

## Buy new or used appliances?

If broken clothes washers cannot be easily repaired, our policy is to replace them with a quality used one, or with lower end new appliances (like the Kenmore brand from Sears). At a used appliance store that we frequent, not only do they recondition used appliances, they include a six month warranty.

Once we bought a washer and dryer from a

*craigslist.com* advertisement. We had to drive 15 miles (one way) to pick them up then haul them back to our rental house in our truck. We installed them and they seemed to work alright. But, a few days after the tenants had moved in, they reported that the washer was leaking oil and the dryer was burning their clothes.

Long story short, we had to buy another washer and dryer, this time at the appliance store, to replace the original ones. It was a loss of time and money to buy two sets of appliances, but we learned a good lesson. We had purchased appliances that were too old, and we didn't check them out thoroughly enough.

**Buy bargain appliances before you need them**

Despite that setback with the washer, we think that *Craigslist* and yard sales are still great places to pick up good used appliances at great prices. If we see a nice working appliance for a good price, or something else that we anticipate that we could use in a rental house, we will purchase it, even though we don't have any immediate need for it. We'll just store it in our shed until we need it.

We bought a used furnace at a yard sale for only $40 and installed it into a rental house and it has worked great. For furnaces, there are very few moving parts to worry about, and the electrical wiring is relatively simple. As long as the motor is in good operating condition, you're home free.

We once literally picked up a clothes dryer from the side of the road that had a "Free Dryer" sign taped to it. We gave it a new home and it has been working reliably for over 10 years now. The only repair, about five years ago, was that we had to change the on/off switch on the door.

**Step 4: Simplify landscaping**

The front yard of your rental houses must look great. Curb appeal gives the potential tenants a good first impression. Simple and neat landscaping gives the tenant comfort that the yard is low maintenance and low in water consumption; saving the tenants money on water and saving you time later not having to replace a yard full of dead plants.

We personally like to utilize decorative rocks on our rental yards, and plants that don't require any watering, like *Mesquite* and *Palo Verde* trees, which have long roots that tap into the aquifer.

### Step 5:  Re-key the locks

One other thing that we like to do before a new tenant moves in is to re-key all the locks. This is cheaper than buying new doorknobs, and it provides security for our tenants. This protects you and your tenants in case a previous tenant has surreptitiously kept an extra copy of a house key.

Now your house has passed inspection and is standing at attention, eagerly waiting to be rented out. At ease, Private. Let's look at how to get tenants.

### 7 steps to attract tenants to your house like a tractor beam

The Imperial Battlestation *Death Star I* was armed with 768 Phylon tractor beams enabling it to constrain the *Millennium Falcon*, but for attracting tenants to your rental property quickly and as inexpensively as possible, we will arm you with only the following 7 steps.

### Step 1:  For rent sign

Install a "For Rent" sign in the front yard of the property, where it can be easily seen from the street. We buy one of the large red and white signs with a sturdy metal frame that are available at most hardware stores. The most important feature is that the sign must be clearly visible and easy to read.

Place your contact phone number in large, clear letters on the sign using large stick-on numbers to increase readability. If potential tenants are forced to get out of their car because they can't read your phone number, they may just decide to keep on driving rather than getting out. Make it as easy as possible for weekend rental searches to get this necessary information.

### Step 2:  Advertise on Craigslist

List your property on *craigslist.org*. In today's computerized world, many people start their search for a rental home online. We have had good responses from using the free advertisements on *craigslist*.

In most cases, we do not recommend using the newspaper to advertise. In our opinion, newspapers have gone the way of the bell bottom pants and the lava lamp. Most people get their information from other sources. Newspapers are too expensive and less effective than other techniques that are free.

### Step 3: Make a flyer

Make a one-page flyer that describes your rental property. Pick a few pictures that highlight your home to potential tenants. Create the flyer on your computer. Incorporate your photos, the rental address, your contact information, monthly rental cost, and your phone number. List all house amenities, number of beds & baths, school district, A/C, garage descriptions, pets allowed, and new appliances. Also, mention any nearby stores that would be convenient for tenants.

Anticipate and address questions in the flyer that people may have about your property. You do not want to waste your time, or theirs, with needless calls for additional information.

We tape copies of the flyer to the front windows of our property.

We also attach a tube to our For Rent sign in the front yard so people can take a flyer. We make sure that we have flyers inside the house to hand out to everyone who comes to see the house. Many people look at several houses on the same day, during their rental search, so a flyer helps them remember the key details of our home.

### Step 4: Make room for pets

We like to rent out our houses to people who have pets. It increases the amount of the tenant applications, and we think we get more stable tenants in the property if they can have their pets. Many people consider their pet a member of their family, and in some cases, make their decision on which home to rent based on the likely comfort of their pet.

Maybe pet owners cross the line when they refer to themselves as "mommy" and "daddy," but that's okay.

Many people will not live in a property that doesn't allow pets. We accommodate them by allowing tenants to have small pets and we charge $10 a month for each pet. Small pets include dogs below 20-25 pounds (no dangerous breeds), cats, and birds. (We charge extra for bird-zillas over 25 pounds!). It's a win-win situation. The tenants have a nice place to stay with their pets, and we are able to make a little extra money each month.

If the pets destroy something (e.g., the carpet, fence, or screen door), we just use the money from the tenant's security deposit to make the repairs.

## Liability issues with pets

Are landlords liable if a tenant's dog bites someone? According to *NOLO, Law for All*, courts hold a landlord liable only if the landlord:

1.) Knew the dog was dangerous and could have had the dog removed; or

2.) "Harbored" or "kept" the tenant's dog-that is, cared for or had some control over the dog. (http://www.nolo.com/legal-encyclopedia/free-books/dog-book/chapter4-7.html)

In other words, under normal circumstances, if a tenant's dog escaped from the rental property and you were not aware that the dog was dangerous; the tenant would be considered liable. However, if you knew the dog was dangerous and the dog bites someone, then you could be held liable, or if you yourself were taking care of the dog.

## Step 5: Plant your arrow signs

Place "For Rent" signs on street corners in the neighborhood around your house. Find a high traffic street near your home, and place a ground-staked sign with your address there. The signs should be placed near the road, and not on private property. Any other area that you deem a valuable marketing place should also be adorned with a "For Rent" sign to attract as many people as possible.

We use short arrow signs (from hardware stores) to point people to our house. They are fairly inexpensive and small, and they can be placed almost anywhere without being obnoxious. People may remove or knock down larger signs, but these shorter signs seem to stay up longer.

## Step 6: Open houses

To reduce the amount of time that we need to spend showing the property, we offer "Open House" hours on the weekends. An example of Open House hours would be from 9-12 on Saturdays and 1-4 on Sundays. We put an Open House sign next to our For Rent sign to draw people in.

We just tell callers the weekend Open House hours and inform them that we will be showing the home and handing out applications. This solves the problem of unnecessary trips across town to the rental property every time someone calls and wants to see it.

Contrary to what many house seekers may think, we don't just stare at the phone at night, waiting for someone to call and say "we just love the rental house and would like to see it right away." Not so fast there, Speedy. We have a life too, you know.

## Step 7: Piggyback with apartment finders

There are companies that help tenants find rental properties. They are glad to find new properties to show their clients and will promote your property for no charge. Yes, we said for no charge.

The companies go by the name "Tucson Apartment Finder" or "Tucson Apartment Guide." Although they usually have the word "apartment" in the name, they list rental houses as well. Contact these companies, if they don't contact you first. They will funnel more tenants to your property.

In the next chapter we will examine our virtually infallible process for selecting the best tenants

# Chapter 3:  Selecting Tenants

The number one reason that most people do not want to own rental properties is because they "are afraid of getting bad tenants." You can avoid this problem by utilizing a tested tenant selection process. Follow these 5 steps and you will greatly increase your odds for getting good tenants.

### 5 steps to get good tenants

### Step 1 - The flyer:  the first screening device

Yes, we described the basics for creating a flyer in the previous chapter. But now, we take the humble flyer one step further and add yet another task for it to accomplish.

Of course your flyer is an advertisement, but it should be worded to target and attract the clientele you are looking for. By simply stating the price and security deposit that you require you quickly weed out the people who simply can't afford to rent your property.

If you state that this is a "no smoking" property, and no large animals are allowed, many people will be able to further eliminate themselves.

Furthermore, stating that you will run a credit check and criminal background check on the applicants (whether you actually do so or not) will winnow out even more undesirable applications.

The key is to give people enough information so that people can eliminate themselves before they ever think about calling and pestering you. We have got telemarketers who do that for us.

## Step 2 - First meeting or contact

Probably, your first contact with the prospective tenant will be by telephone, although it could be at the property itself. Either way, you need to have your talking points ready, so that you can quickly but comprehensively describe the property and the lease arrangements.

You want to cover such things as location, amenities, rental cost, and security deposit. Put the property in the best possible light, but also describe the high expectations that you have for tenants.

You should prepare a set of questions that you would like to ask the prospective tenant. Ask questions about their reason for moving, employment, date required and length of stay, number of people, children, pets, smoking, and credit strength. Be alert for any answers that may indicate "red flags."

If anyone doesn't want to answer your questions, or becomes agitated or annoyed, you probably won't want them as a tenant, since you are asking them in a polite and non-threatening manner.. A serious tenant will be happy to answer all the questions correctly and completely. The information that you get will be an aid when you make your final tenant selection.

If you have a "bad feeling" about someone, heed the warning to weed out applications that seem weird, strange, off, or otherwise not right. If a tenant only refers to their self in the third person ("Sam likes the house." "Sam would like to rent the house"), that would be a little too creepy for us. Just be careful not to discriminate against tenants on the basis of race, creed, or color. (More on that a little later.)

When talking to potential tenants, share information about yourself to build up trust with them. Asking someone about their hobbies, or telling them about yours, is a good way to establish rapport with them. Try to get a feel for whether or not they will be someone that you would like to have living in your rental home.

## Trust your intuition

For example, in one house that we own, we were having an open house and a man and woman came in to look at the house. The woman was talkative and friendly, but the man was quiet and didn't allow us to engage him in conversation. We had a bad feeling that we would have a hard time dealing with this guy.

When we got their application, it confirmed our feelings even more when we saw that he had only filled in about half the application. Our first thought was, what does he have to hide? Even though the guy owned a business and made good money, we didn't want him as a tenant because we didn't trust him. Our sixth sense was tingling. So we rented to another couple that was more approachable.

### Step 3 – Showing the property and evaluating tenants at the same time

A good thing to do when people come to look at the property is to allow them to wander around and explore the unit by themselves. This gives people time to imagine what it would be like to live their life in that home; what it will feel like to return from work and relax in the family area; what meals they could cook in the kitchen; which is the best wall to hang their *Starry Night* print. That is what we prefer when we are looking at properties.

It's distracting to have someone follow us around and

point out every feature of the house. You probably know how it is to be herded through a viewing by an overzealous host.

"And this is the kitchen!" says the real estate agent.

"Could have fooled me," we say under our breath (channeling David Spade).

"Oh, we see. That's why there is an oven and frig in here," we silently mutter.

But in case the potential tenants have questions, be ready to respond. That is the time to emphasize the good points of the property. This is an opportune time to engage them in conversation and find out a little more about them. Get that good feeling that was described above.

For example, ask them, what's their favorite movie? If the answer is *The Wizard of Oz*, get them to sign the rental agreement as quickly as possible. If their favorite movie is *Battlefield Earth*, well, you might want to ask them if the neighbor's bagpipe music will be a problem and make a note to do an additional background check.

## Step 4 - The tenant application form

The more information you have on the prospect, the easier it is to make a decision on whether or not to select them as a tenant. You must use a comprehensive tenant application form for them to fill out. Tell the prospect it is very important that all sections of the form are completed and every adult occupant must be listed on the form.

The reason this is so important is the application form is a permanent record of the tenant's declaration as to, employment history, income status, references, and other personal details such as do they smoke, have pets or will there be additional occupants, and children. We usually get a copy of the tenants" driver's license as proof of their identity.

This form is also an important document because it is a crucial component of the tenant screening process.

We have included a sample tenant application form in the Appendix.

## Background checks

Performing a background check is a way to verify that the impressions you have of your applicants are true. Everyone who wants to rent a house has to fill out an application form. We will select the best candidate, based on the processes mentioned above, and then call all the references and former landlords listed on the application form.

Always try to verify the references by telephone. It has been our experience people will often give candid opinions when you ask them. Do beware. You wouldn't be the first landlord to be given a fake reference.

An applicant once put down Thurston Howell as a reference. We knew that was false right away, because we also knew Thurston Howell had been lost and stranded on *Gilligan's Island* for three seasons.

We don't run credit checks, but we do like to see copies of their paystubs. We do a criminal background check by searching county court house records, and we also check the sex offender's registry list.

A high priority for us is that they make enough money to pay the rent. Don't go by what they say; go by what their paycheck says.

## Stop blabbing and just show us the money!

Here is a true story that has repeated itself many

times over the course of our being landlords. Only the names and the faces change.

A prospective tenant says, "So anyhoo! Don't worry about the monthly rental payments. We've got that covered. We operate a great business selling unique t-shirts on *eBay*."

In our minds we're thinking, "Hello! Is anybody in there? (We imagine rapping their cranium with a rubber-headed mallet.) Unless you are selling Kim Kardashian *in* a *Purple Rain* t-shirt, selling t-shirts on *eBay* is not a steady income. Come back when your paycheck is signed by Saint Laurent."

Do we really say that? No. The words that actually come out of our mouths are, "Okaaay. We have a lot of applications to rent this house. We'll let you know if you are selected. Thank you for coming by."

## Step 5 - Selecting your tenant - the crucial decision

Tell your prospective renter that it's very important for the information on the application form be complete and accurate. They must fill in all the blanks. And do a quick reality check for yourself. Look for signs and inconsistencies in the information given. Does it all add up?

Watch out for misinformation from an existing or recent landlord. The landlord might be fed up with the tenant and will give an overly positive reference just to get rid of his problem tenant. You are likely to get a more realistic account from a previous landlord - the one before the current one.

## The tenant selection rating sheet

We have used two ways to evaluate tenants. These are:

1.) The simple way. We just accumulate as many applications as we can, then pick the best one based on our impression of the application, and our tuition of how happy we would be with this tenant living in our rental house.

2.) The systematic way. We assign numbers to various categories that rate the applicant, and then we add up the numbers and pick the applicant with the highest grade. We learned this system from long-time real estate investor and friend, Connie Brzowski.

## Never discriminate but establish criteria

The *Fair Housing Act* says,

*No person shall be subjected to discrimination because of race, color, religion, sex, disability, familial status, age, or national origin.*

While you cannot discriminate on the above criteria, you can base decisions on almost any other criteria. This includes such things as ability to pay, personality traits, cleanliness, criminal background, and anything else that you feel would disqualify them from being a good tenant.

The systematic approach is a little more scientific and it provides us some protection if someone ever questions our compliance with the *Fair Housing Act*.

Here are some of the criteria that we have in our Tenant Selection Rating Sheet.

**Minimum selection criteria:**

1.) Must have verifiable monthly income of at least 3 times the rent
2.) Must be able to provide a photo ID – preferably a driver's license
3.) Must have no felony convictions

During the interview and when showing the house:

1.) Must show punctuality
2.) Must be respectful and courteous
3.) Must be neat and clean in appearance

**Must have for the application:**

1.) Attached copies of ID to application (Driver's license and Social security card)
2.) Filled out application entirely leaving no blanks
3.) Able to pay first month's rent and security deposit
4.) Proof of stable income or employment

We have included the complete 2-page version of the *Tenant Selection Rating Sheet* in the Appendix. It allows you to assign points to each line. Then you can add up the numbers and select the best tenant based on the high score.

### Step 6 - Signing the Agreement

We usually sign the agreement at the property that the tenants are going to rent. We cover three things with them at the signing:

1.) We read through the entire contract together to answer any questions and to ensure there are no misunderstandings.

2.) We collect the first month's rent along with their security deposit.

3.) We conduct a property walk-through with the Property Inspection Sheet in hand, and the tenants and us both sign the sheet confirming that everything is in good condition. Or, if there is anything in need of repair, these are noted. (See The Appendix for a copy of the Property Inspection Sheet that we use.)

## Leases and contracts

There are two common types of leases:

1.) The yearly lease and;

2.) The month-to-month lease.

You may think that it makes good business sense to commit a tenant for a year (or more) in a yearly lease, but at the same time you are also committing yourself. It is much harder to remove a problem tenant when you are both committed to a yearly lease. From our experience, we have settled on using a month-to-month lease for almost all our tenants. This allows us to have the upper hand in removing a problem tenant. If you have a tenant that you want to get rid of, it's much easier to do if they are on a month to month lease.

We are not trying to frighten you, and the reality is

there are many great tenants, but you also need to protect yourself from tenants with bad habits, who:

1.) Disturb the neighbors;
2.) Take no pride in caring for the house; or
3.) Are consistently delinquent in their payment.

With a month-to-month leasing agreement, you can just cancel the contract with a notification to the tenants that they must be out in 30 days. No confrontations. No messy court fights

This is your rental property; therefore you are in control of the agreement. Feel free to modify a contract to make the tenants behave the way that you want them to. Nothing is set in stone. It's your contract. Mold it into something that works.

We have constantly molded and improved our contract. Here are some of the key components that our lease includes:

1.) Tenants are responsible for paying the utilities, the (electricity, gas and water). If the landlord pays any utilities you are encouraging the tenants to be wasteful;
2.) Tenants cannot paint the house or make any significant changes to the landscaping without permission;
3.) No smoking is allowed inside the house; and,
4.) Tenants must maintain outdoor plants.

See the Appendix for a copy of the month-to-month contract that we use, and for the complete list of restrictions that we include in our contract.

## Provide tenants with a list of useful information about the house

We provide our tenants a page that lists things that they will need to know, like the trash pickup schedule, how often to change furnace filters, emergency phone number, electrical switch box, emergency water shut off valve locations, rental check due date, and our phone number and PO Box address where rental checks are mailed. (See the Appendix for a copy of the move in information sheet that we provide to tenants.)

If your house was built before 1977 you must also provide the tenants with a lead-based paint pamphlet to warn them of the dangers of lead-based paint. You can download a copy at:

*http://www.hud.gov/offices/lead/leadhelp.cfm*

How do you maintain good relations with your good tenants?

Respect their space. Respond promptly to maintenance calls. Don't sweat the small stuff with your good tenants. The foremost goal is to keep them in your property as long as you can. More on this in the next chapter.

# Chapter 4
# Take Care of Tenants to Increase Profits

If your goal, like ours, is to become, not a mediocre or merely a good, but a great landlord (an award which has thus far eluded us), then you must focus like *Arjuna* (the legendary archer who never missed a target) on the wellbeing of your tenants.

How should your treat tenants? The best way is to just treat tenants the way that you would like to be treated. Think about it. At some point we have all probably been tenants. When we were tenants, we expected the landlord to quickly respond to our calls to report something was broke or malfunctioning in the house. We shuttered at the thought of a rate increase, and we all wanted to feel that the place we were renting was really our home sweet home.

But not all tenants will be as chipper as *SpongeBob SquarePants*. You're bound to get an occasional *Squidward* (a topic that we will discuss later), however for the most part tenants can be expected to meet their part of the agreement, and they deserve to be treated as honored guests.

Here are our

**5 crucial tips on how to keep good tenants.**

### 1.) Practice good communication

One of the great pet peeves of tenants is a landlord who is as slow as Christmas in responding to their needs.

Does it take you 2 hours to watch the television show *60 Minutes*?

Then maybe you're too slow.

If you are slow to respond to your tenant requests for

help, you will be perceived as uncaring. This can lead to bad relations with your tenants, and may eventually result in your tenants moving away to another property.

Any time a tenant calls us and leaves a message, we immediately return their call even if it is only to touch base to let them know we received their call. When we are working a regular 8:00 to 5:00 job, we can still manage our rental house business by having a cell phone with us everywhere we go. This way, we can deal quickly with tenant issues that may become exponentially worse like a broken water pipe, or some similar circumstance that can lead to property damage or even worse, injury to someone.

## Use memos instead of phone calls

A phone call is good when you need to quickly get in contact with your tenant, but if it's not an urgent matter our preferred means of communication with tenants is by sending them memos by regular mail.

There are times when written communication and notifications are absolutely essential. For example, if the tenant is not keeping up the yard work around their rental property, as agreed upon in the rental contract, we will write them a note in a calm and respectful manner identifying the problem. We may make a reference to the section of the contract that requires them to keep up the yard (but only if they are a repeat offender), and describe what needs to be performed to meet the terms of the agreement. (See the Appendix for the sample letter that we sent a tenant to remind them about yard work.)

A phone call could easily turn into a heated conversation, but with a memo, the tone stays calm and the point gets made. In addition, we have a written record of what we have told them that we keep in the tenant's file folder.

We keep our tenants informed about activities that we have planned for their property. We will usually call and let them know well ahead of time if we plan to do some preventative maintenance on the roof, for example. If a plumber cancels an appointment, we'll call them so they are not waiting around all afternoon for no reason. It's really just practicing common courtesy.

## 2.) Timely responses to repair requests

We admit that when we first became landlords in 2002, this was a low priority for us. We used to cringe when we'd answer the phone and a tenant would be on the line with a repair request. We knew we were going to have to spend some of our valuable time and hard-earned money to deal with a maintenance request. We would sometimes let the repair linger instead of jumping right on it.

Now, we look at tenant calls as an opportunity to show the tenants that we take their problems seriously, and we respond to their concerns immediately. We have busy schedules, but our tenants have busy schedules too.

Keeping our good tenants happy is our highest priority because it directly affects our profits. The fewer tenant turnovers that we have the more money we make.

## Put "Who you gonna call?" list on speed dial

What has helped us to respond quickly is that we now have accumulated a "Who you gonna call?" list of good repair professionals over time.

We have plumbers, an air conditioner company,

handymen, Ghostbusters, Chuck Norris, and other professionals that we trust, on the speed dial of our cell phone. That way, we can get them started on a repair without delay.

### 3.) Protecting tenant privacy

This issue is really close to our heart. Shorty after we were married, we were on sort of a working honeymoon in Mexico. We rented a house near the beach and after we were there a few days, we mentioned to the landlord that the sink was draining too slowly.

The next day was Saturday, and we still in bed that morning. Angy was sleeping and Terry was reading *The Hitchhikers Guide to the Galaxy*, when we heard the back door opening. It sounded like two people were entering.

A happy *SpongeBob*-ish called out, "We're here to fix the sink."

Terry yelled, "Hey, why are you guys here so early? We're still in bed."

The *SpongeBob* voice said, "Sorry, we have a tight schedule to keep. It's not easy being a handyman you know."

"What did he say?" whispered Angy.

"He said its not easy being a handyman."

"Well, that's his problem isn't it?"

"I would have thought so."

Terry shouted out, "Can you guys come back later? We're not prepared right now. And if you could avoid unloading your burdens on us we'd really appreciate it."

"Come on," said the cheerful voice, "we can fix this pipe in two shakes." We could hear random tools dropping on the floor and bouncing around, followed by an exclamation of "Oops."

"And we are really good guys. I read poetry and I'm good at carrying on interesting conversations."

"And, I write novels," the other one with a goofy, *Patrick*-ish voice chimed in, "although I haven't had any published yet."

Objections to the contrary, we had our sink fixed and the handymen did turn out to be pretty good guys. They became our friends over the course of our stay.

Although this was just a light hearted incident, it was also an example of violation of tenants' privacy. Not only is it wrong from a courtesy perspective, but it is also against the law to enter the premises without the tenant's permission, except in an emergency.

The more you can make the tenants feel it is their home, like keeping a handyman poet and a Pulitzer Prize wannabe from showing up unannounced to their private living space, the better your relationship with them will be.

## 4.) Rental fee increases

We know that many landlords feel the need to regularly raise tenant rental fees. For obvious reasons, this can stir up the resentment of tenants and may cause them to think about looking for a new property.

We don't have this problem because the only time we raise rents are when one tenant moves out and another one moves in. Our philosophy is, why give the tenants any reason to look for another place to live?

In the case of rent increases for extremely long-term tenants, we think that tenants don't mind paying a fair and competitive price, as long as it doesn't seem like an exorbitant increase to them. Sensitivity is the key in this situation. A memo may not suffice. You may need to have a heart to heart discussion with the tenants at the time of the rental contract renewal.

## 5.) Keeping tenants satisfied = more $ for your

Putting the comfort of your tenants first results in you making more money. Three things happen when you increase the value (or usefulness) of a property:

1.) You attract more and better tenants;

2.) Tenants stay longer; and,

3.) You make more money.

Some things that you can do to make a property more valuable include:

1.) Put a in clothes washer and dryer;

2.) Have a refrigerator;

3.) Add a carport to protect tenant cars from the sun;

4.) Install security doors;

5.) Put a storage shed in the back yard;

6.) Allow pets, as mentioned earlier.

These things all increase the value of a property for both you and the tenants, and may set your property far apart from other rental properties that may appear similar in quality or are found in the same neighborhood. Added value to the house puts the house in a higher price bracket and justifies you in asking for a higher monthly rent. And, the more satisfied a tenant is, the more likely they are willing to pay a little extra rent.

Good tenants are to be relished and pampered. Bad tenants require an entirely different strategy. Just follow our suggestions in the next chapter and you can easily divest yourself of these unwanted reprobates.

Turn Your Home Into a Rental House Instead of Selling It!

## Chapter 5
## Dealing with Problem Tenants

Most tenants are real pleasures to do business with. You rarely even hear a single complaint or a peep from them. They see the rental unit as their home and a reflection of themselves, and they go the extra mile to maintain your property and get along beautifully with the neighbors. They're like Homer Simpson's neighbor, Ned Flanders.

On the opposite end of the spectrum, there are tenants who require constant attention and supervision, like a young *Dennis the Menace* who incessantly tests our limits.

Casey Stengel, former manager of the *New York Yankees* baseball team, said that his philosophy of coaching was, "to keep those players who hate me away from those who are still undecided." As landlords, we want to keep the bad tenants, who probably hate us if we are doing our job right, away from our rental properties.

Here are the most common tenant-related problems that landlords may face:

1.) Tenants that pay late or don't pay;

2.) Noisy tenants;

3.) Messy or destructive tenants.

With practice, a good contract, along with a good reference book that includes legal forms, these problems can be fairly easily managed. Like learning to ride a unicycle, it does take some time and experience to be a good landlord. You may fall down and scrape your knee a few times, but you have to actually deal with a few tenants to become really good at it.

Don't get discouraged if you get stuck with a problem tenant, and you feel at loss that you don't know for sure what to do. It's all part of the learning process. As for us, we actually thought of giving up the renal house business during the first couple of years because of trouble with tenants. But, looking back, we can see that those early difficulties allowed us to develop the "landlording" skills needed for long term success.

A book that has helped us greatly is the *Arizona Landlords' Deskbook* by Carlton Casler. This book has all the right legal forms and sensible advice on how to deal with problem tenants, so that everything is done according to the letter of the law. It is particularly useful in the discussions of proper screening of tenants and eviction procedures. The forms provided are very helpful and designed to be photocopied and used for your tenants.

There are other similar legal-type guides, such as *California Landlord's Law Book: Rights & Responsibilities* published by Ingram Pub Services, and NOLO's *Every Landlord's Legal Guide* by attorneys Janet Portman, Marcia Stewart, and Ralph Warner. We encourage you to find a book like one of these (preferably dealing with your state) that cover the legal aspects of being a landlord, and which includes the useful landlord forms.

## Handling difficult situations

As tempting as it may be, do not procrastinate when it comes to handling difficult situations, or making tough decisions. Nothing is gained when problems are swept under a rug. Yes, sometimes finding a new, and problem free tenant will be required, but it's better to replace a bad tenant than to jeopardize your investment property.

As we mentioned, the absolute best way to deal with bad tenants that you need to get rid of is to rent your property on a month-to-month lease. In this way, both the tenant and the landlord have the option to cancel the contract at any time. If it gets to the point where eviction is called for, you just give the tenant a one month written notice, and they are out of your hair by the next month.

You don't even need to have a good reason to remove a problem tenant. You are just exercising your right to cancel their monthly contract. It removes the need to go to court to kick out a problem tenant. Easy as pie.

Here are five steps that we suggest you follow to remove a problem tenant:

1.) Tenant engages in some action that violates the contract, for example, they pay the rent late.

2.) Call the tenants to inform them they are in violation of the contract.

3.) Follow up immediately with a memo to restate that they have violated the contract, and tell them exactly what you expect them to do. For example, they need to pay the rent at a specified date. Tell them the consequences of not immediately remedying the situation. For example if they don't pay the rent, you will terminate the month-to-month contract.

4.) If they don't take the appropriate action, of if another violation occurs; send them a form stating that you are cancelling the contract. They must be out in 30 days.

5.) If they are not out in 30 days, you can pay a fee to have a deputy sheriff evict them ($300 in our city). If they are still behind on their rent when they leave, you can keep their security deposit to cover the cost the rent.

But don't get the impression that the renal business is fraught with eviction notices. Most of our tenants have been good tenants. We have only had one eviction in the 10 years that we have operated our business. And in that case, the month-to-month lease made that eviction a fairly easy process.

## Should you use a management company?

While we prefer to manage our properties ourselves, hiring a management company is an option that many investors consider. Companies will generally charge you 10% of the rent that they collect.

However, the unvarnished truth is that no company will manage your property as well as you would yourself. They may have hundreds of properties that they are managing, so individual properties may not get much personal attention. If this is the course you take, we encourage you to shop around for a good company. Ask other investors what companies they use.

Another option is to train a trustworthy individual to manage your properties. This reduces the cost over hiring a management company, and increases the amount of care and attention that your properties will receive. It's a little less conventional, but we know people who have done it and are pleased with the results.

# Chapter 6
# The Secret to Increasing Cash Flow - Invest in Transition Zones

Francis Bacon said "A wise man will make more opportunities than he finds." For real estate investors, one of the best places to find opportunity is in areas that we call "transition zones."

Don't just find houses that meet your criteria, find the house that meets your criteria in locations where people like to rent. There are nice areas in our town and there are not-so-nice areas in our town. However, neither of those two areas is where most people like to rent properties.

There is a "transition" zone between the nice and not-so-nice areas where people are eager to rent, and where house values are relatively lower, and these are areas where you can charge a moderately high rent. You will find there are both good and bad houses in these zones, and usually there are supermarkets and stores within walking distance.

## Advantages of transition zones

Transition zones have one overriding advantage over other areas of town: you can make more money with them. There are two reasons for this:

1.) You pay less for a rental property in a transition zone than you would for a comparable property in a nicer neighborhood.

2.) You can charge about the same rent as you would in a nice neighborhood.

For example, we own two houses in two different parts of the city. We have one house in a nicer neighborhood on the edge of town where new growth is taking place. We pay $700 for the mortgage, and we receive $875 in rent for a profit of $185/month.

We own a second house in a transition zone neighborhood, near the central part of town where property values are lower. For this house, we pay $525 for the mortgage, receive $750 for rent, and turn a $250/month rental profit.

It is not how much we make each month for a house, but how little we pay for the mortgage that accounts for the higher transition zone profit!

## Why do people live in transition zones?

1.) Amenities are close by. Transition zone properties are usually within walking distance of bus stops, groceries and drug stores.

2.) Lower reliance on cars. Many people want to reduce, or even eliminate, their dependence on the automobile.

## Our transition zone experience

We bought our first family home in a transition zone. The price was right and the property was located close to stores and services, and we also walked around the neighborhood at night for exercise.

The area was a mixture of all types of housing. In a four square block area where we lived there were owner-occupied homes, townhouses, apartments, and trailer parks. Our house was located within three blocks of two grocery stores, a video rental store, a 7-11 and Circle K stores, an auto parts store, a Taco Bell, a McDonald's, and a pharmacy.

Granted, the area had some rough edges and maybe a few strange characters in the neighborhood. But they were in the minority. (We don't mean scary strange characters like Freddy Krueger or Lex Luthor; but curiously strange characters like Edward Scissorhands or Conan O'Brien).

After we lived in that first house for nine years, we bought another house and kept our first house as a rental. We recently bought a second house in the same transition zone as the first house that we owned. One of the great benefits of owning rental houses in this "transition zone" area is that it is very easy to find good tenants.

# Turn Your Home Into a Rental House Instead of Selling It!

## Chapter 7
## Property Inspection and Due Diligence

Buying fixer-upper houses, living in them, repairing them, and eventually renting them out is a safe way to generate short-term income and long-term wealth.

Even Arnold Schwarzenegger, in his book *Total Recall*, cites investing in real estate as a valuable step on his road to financial success.

But, how can you be sure that a house is worth what you are offering to pay for it? Based on experience, we can "eyeball" the property and probably be able to make a pretty accurate estimate of its worth, maybe 75% of the time

That's probably closer to 95% of the time for Arnold, with that Terminator vision of his.

### Get a professional inspection

However, that's not good enough. We need more information than our educated eyeball can provide in order to:

1.) Avoid any surprise defects. After you buy the property, trying to get reimbursed for those defects will be too late.

2.) Negotiate a lower selling price for the house.

We hire a professional inspector to do a thorough physical and structural inspection, and to provide us with a complete written inspection report. The inspector's report is a great tool to help us negotiate a lower price on the house if they uncover anything that is in need of repair. Hiring a qualified property inspector is a good way to make sure that we are really getting what you pay for in a house.

## The "due diligence" period

Once you have made an offer on a house and it has been accepted by the seller, the "due diligence" period begins. You have until the close of escrow (or completion of the sale) to check out the physical and financial condition of the property. If you discover that the property has problems that were not apparent earlier, but you think the deal is still worth pursuing, the seller may be willing to correct any deficiencies, or give you money to complete the necessary work yourself.

## The key components of due diligence

1.) Review of books and records
In our case, there are usually no records to review. Most of the houses that we buy have been repossessed by a bank, the *Veterans Administration*, or the *U.S. Department of Housing and Urban Development* (HUD), and the owner is long gone. However, if they are available, you should get copies of:

a.) the owner's *Schedule E* from their federal taxes to verify profit and loss (if it was a rental);

b.) information on improvements (to verify code compliance) or maintenance (including termite control) done to the property; and

c.) any files on tenants who are still living in the property.

2.) The physical inspection

When there is no owner present this makes the

physical inspection all the more important. When having the physical inspection done, make sure to be aware of the most common house problems.

## Ten most frequent house problems

A survey of U.S. home inspectors resulted in this list of the most frequently encountered problems in the homes they have inspected (Blue Ribbon Home Warranty Survey Results, 2012).

1.) Improper Surface Grading/Drainage
This is responsible for the most common of household maladies: water penetration of the basement or crawl space.

2.) Improper Electrical Wiring
Includes such situations as insufficient electrical service to the house, inadequate overload protection, and amateur, often dangerous, wiring connections.

3.) Roof Damage
Involves roof leakage, caused by old or damaged shingles or improper flashing.

4.) Heating Systems
Problems in this category include broken or malfunctioning heating and air conditioning controls, blocked chimneys, and unsafe discharge of exhaust.

5.) Poor Overall Maintenance
Demonstrated by such signs as cracked, peeling, or dirty

painted surfaces, crumbling masonry, makeshift wiring or plumbing, and broken fixtures or appliances.

6.) Structural Problems
Many houses, as a result of problems in one or more of the other categories, sustain damage to such structural components as foundation walls, floor joists, rafters, window and door frames.

7.) Plumbing
Problems consist of the existence of old or incompatible piping materials, as well as faulty fixtures and waste lines.

8.) Exteriors
Flaws in a home's exterior, including windows, doors, and wall surfaces, are responsible for the discomfort of water and air penetration. Inadequate caulking and/or weather-stripping are the most common culprits.

9.) Poor Ventilation
Due to overly ambitious efforts to save energy, many home owners have "over-sealed" their homes, resulting in excessive interior moisture. This can cause rotting and premature failure of both structural and non-structural elements.

10.) Miscellaneous
Includes primarily interior components, often cosmetic in nature. May include dents in doors and walls from children's unsupervised indoor karate practice (in our case). We learned this one the hard way.

A home inspector's standard practice typically does not include the following, for which a specific license to inspect and identify is required:

- Asbestos
- Radon Gas
- Lead Paint
- Toxic Mold
- Pest Control

If you suspect the presence of any of these items, you must contract with inspectors in these areas independently.

## Importance of Disclosure

Hidden defects, those which are not visible to the naked eye, are only identified through delving deep into the bowels of the house where few have treaded. Some potential problems, such a water pipes imbedded in the slab would be nearly impossible to evaluate. In fact, you couldn't evaluate it at all unless you had a disclosure from the seller

You will never discover some of the problems that exist unless the seller tells you, which is what disclosure is all about.

## The Tucson Police example

The concept of disclosure reminds us of when the Tucson police were looking for a man they suspected of a string of burglaries. They had six photographs of the man, all taken in different locations and from different angles. They sent faxes of the pictures to police departments all over the country.

Three days later, Tucson received a fax from the police chief from a small town in Arizona. The report read, "We got right to work on those six pictures you sent. We've arrested five of the suspects, and we have the sixth under observation right now."

This was classic case of a cloud of confusion caused by not enough disclosure.

## Take the moral high road

Many states have seller disclosure requirements for residential renal property with four or fewer units. Sellers are required to supply the buyer with a written statement that identifies all known structural and mechanical problems, and in many cases, the seller must complete a comprehensive questionnaire.

Our opinion is that whether or not a formal disclosure statement is required, if you are the seller, it is in your best interest to disclose all problems that could affect the value or use of the house. Two reasons to fully disclose problems are:

1) morally, it is the right thing to do, and

2) the buyer could still come back and take you to court under claims of misrepresentation and fraud.

Why take the chance? Once you sell a house, you and look for another property. You want to be done with it and not have to worry about being dragged into court.

Remember, whether or not there is a disclosure, the due diligence period is your last opportunity to either:

1.) Complete the transaction, or

2.) Cancel the escrow, have your money returned, and look for another rental house.

## Inspect the inspectors before you hire one

Many investors hire a property inspector based on the advice of a real estate agent, which is not necessarily a bad way to go. But, you will be spending a tidy sum to hire an inspector, so it's best to interview a few before deciding. You may see a big difference in experience, qualifications, and ethical standards.

We would never hire an inspector who would not allow us to accompany him during the inspection. Tagging along with the inspector presents a great opportunity to learn about your property, and will arm you with knowledge that will be invaluable throughout your entire ownership of the house. Generally, inspectors are happy to have you accompany them.

If you want a true professional, hire a full-time inspector who perform at least 100 inspections a year and who carries "errors and omissions" insurance. This coverage tells you that the person is working full-time in the field and is participating in ongoing continuing education.

To locate certified inspectors and to find out more about the inspection process see the *American Society of Home Inspectors* web page (*http://www.ashi.org/*)

If we haven't used an inspector previously, we ask for a sample of a recent inspection report. And, if you want to get serious about it, you could ask an inspector to provide you contact information for 2 or 3 people who have used their service in the last few months.

Price should be a secondary concern because, like

other professional services, they often pay for themselves. An internet check on inspection costs indicated that prices range from $215 to $750, with an average price of $260.

# Chapter 8
# Follow EPA Renovation Guidelines

Common renovation activities like sanding, cutting, and demolition can create hazardous lead dust and chips by disturbing lead-based paint, which can be harmful to adults and children.

As owners of a relatively small number of rental properties, it may be tempting to think that we are exempt from the regulations that apply to people who own real estate empires. We can just wander into our rental houses, hammer in hand, and do our little renovation projects, right? We are, after all, captains of our own ship, and masters of our own destiny.

Hold on there, Sherlock, EPA begs to differ.

## Get certified or get out of Dodge

Property owners who renovate, repair, or prepare surfaces for painting in pre-1978 rental housing must, before beginning work, provide tenants with a copy of EPA's lead hazard information pamphlet *Renovate Right: Important Lead Hazard Information for Families, Child Care Providers, and Schools*. As owners of these rental properties we must document that we are complying with this requirement. EPA has a sample "pre-renovation disclosure form" to guide us.

As of 2010, property owners who perform these projects in pre-1978 rental housing must be certified and must follow the lead-safe work practices required by EPA's "Renovation, Repair and Remodeling Guidelines."

## 5 steps to take before beginning a project

Property owners who perform renovation, repairs, and painting jobs in rental property should:

1.) Take training to learn how to perform lead-safe work practices.

2. Learn the lead laws that apply to you regarding certification and lead-safe work practices.

3.) Keep records to demonstrate that you and your workers have been trained in lead-safe work practices and that you follow lead-safe work practices on the job. To make recordkeeping easier, you may use the "sample recordkeeping checklist" that EPA has developed to help contractors comply with the renovation recordkeeping requirements.

4.) Read about how to comply with EPA's rule in the EPA *Small Entity Compliance Guide to Renovate Right* (*http://www.epa.gov/lead/pubs/sbcomplianceguide.pdf*)

5.) Read about how to use lead-safe work practices in EPA's *Steps to Lead Safe Renovation, Repair and Painting* (*http://www.epa.gov/getleadsafe/*).

## Do the new rules apply to my project?

The rule must be followed when "repair or maintenance activities disturb more than 6 square feet of paint per room inside, or more than 20 square feet on the exterior of a home or building." Renovation is defined as any activity that disturbs painted surfaces and includes most repair, remodeling, and maintenance activities, including window replacement.

### What is my motivation to comply?

Fines for violating rule requirements can be up to $37,500 per incident, per day.

## What if I hire a contractor?

If you have the work performed by a contractor, you should make sure that contractor has the proper training and certification.

You can verify that a contractor is certified by checking EPA's website (see above) or by calling the National Lead Information Center at 1-800-424-LEAD (5323). You can also ask to see a copy of the contractor's firm certification.

Realtors and property managers should be aware that they are also affected by these EPA regulations.

## You can still do repairs

Don't let these new rules discourage you from doing repairs. Many of the repairs that we make in our rental properties will be small enough that don't require us to follow the new guidelines.

But, for those larger projects, it's not that difficult to just learn the rules and to follow them. Essentially, we are complying with the law to protect the health of both our tenants and ourselves.

Turn Your Home Into a Rental House Instead of Selling It!

76

## Chapter 9
## When Tenants Move Out to Pursue Their "Stairway to Heaven"

Eventually, tenants start singing:

"There's a feeling I get when I look to the west,
and my spirit is crying for leaving."

It quickly dawns on you that either they have been listening to too much Led Zeppelin music, or they are making plans to move away from your property.

If they are planning to move, you will want to make the transition of the tenant out of the house as smooth as possible. The best way to do this is by telling the tenant what you expect from them by giving them a letter that clearly spells out the checkout process. This way we avoid misunderstandings; we are all on the same page, wavelength, sheet of music, or stairway to heaven.

**Move out information letter to tenants**

Some key things that we mention in our letter are:

1.) How much of their security deposit will be returned.

2.) There will need to be a review of their check in sheet (and attach a copy for them).

3.) What you expect in terms of house cleaning.

4.) Reminders to contact the utility companies to disconnect services in their name.

5.) Reminders to cancel newspaper and other subscriptions and to provide the Postal Service with a change of address form.

6.) Reminders to contact us when they are ready for the final house inspection.

7.) A note that if keys are not returned, they will be charged.

8.) Any costs that we must pay to repair the house will be taken out of their security deposit, and we will refund the money due them within 10 days.

**Refunding the security deposit**

In general, we are pretty lenient when it comes to charging tenants for little things on the checklist. If they move out, and they have been good tenants, we are going return to them most, if not all of their security (or damage) deposit back, barring some obvious big broken item.

Our perspective is that we made a lot of money from the tenants over the years, and we don't want them to leave on a sour note just because they thought we might have overcharged them on some ticky-tack repair.

We have included a copy of the letter that we send to our tenants in the Appendix.

# Chapter 10
## Self Reliance

*Within you there is a silence and a sanctuary to which you can retreat at any time and be yourself.*
-- Herman Hesse, *Siddhartha*

What motivates someone to give up a nice peaceful existence and decide to throw themselves into the unpredictable and challenging world of repairing houses and managing tenants?

Obviously, one motivation is the desire to make more money and to provide for our families. But, if it were only about money a much easier trail, albeit less lucrative, would be to take a second job on weekends at Home Depot or Wal-Mart, and draw a steady second pay check.

If we drill down to the bedrock motivation of most people in this business, at the core they have the desire to be self-reliant. They want to make the decisions that determine their fate in life.

### Don't heed the "experts"

The world is full of people who are more than willing to tell us how to live our lives. But, even the advice of experienced people, with vast knowledge and wealth, should be disregarded, with a gentle smile. The self-reliant person receives his guidance from within himself. As Ralph Waldo Emerson says, all guidance from within is "pure and unfiltered." All guidance from others, no matter how well meaning, is based on opinion.

For the most part, people's opinions have no deep roots and are formed as the wind blows and the latest news headlines relate. Most people who live in the world live according to the rules, and seek the rewards, that the world has established. When we live in solitude that Hermann Hesse refers to, we live after our own rules and the rewards we receive go beyond the physical.

## Action is louder than words

Listening to the guidance from within is one thing, putting it into practice is something else. The following story illustrates the difference.

*A man was praying to God and said, "Please God, I really need some money. Let me win the lottery."*

*He got no response.*

*A week later the man said, "God, I really, really need money. Help me to win the lottery.*

*Again, no reply from God.*

*Another week passed, and the man said, "God, what is going on? I've been good. Why can't I win the lottery?"*

*God replied, "Work with me. Buy a lottery ticket."*

## The essence of rental property owners

We were at the *Habitat for Humanity Store* the day before Christmas to buy a toilet for a rental property. (Did we mention that they have a great selection of used building materials?) The guy who helped us load the toilet onto our pick-up told us that he too was a rental property owner and that he had to fix a leaky roof in one of his properties just the day before.

This is the essence of rental property owners. While most people are getting ready to celebrate Christmas, we are out making repairs to rental properties. We felt a sense of kinship with this other fellow (like in the *Sisterhood of the Traveling Pants*), and no sense of regret or desire to be doing something else. Rather, we felt centered and satisfied with a life that we were completely at home with.

Operating a rental house business is not the only answer and maybe not the easiest answer to living a fulfilling and self-directed life. But, it is a business that has proven to work for many people throughout time, and it is something that is accessible to the average person.

It's not hard to get started. If you've ascertained our subtle (as a freight train) message, you know it can be as easy as turning your house into a rental property when you buy a newer house to live in.

Turn Your Home Into a Rental House Instead of Selling It!

# Chapter 11
# Don't Wait Until You Know Everything

*Always bear in mind, that your own resolution to succeed is more important than any other thing.* -- Abraham Lincoln

We think that never selling your home and, instead, turning it into a rental property is the ideal business for anyone who wants to generate another income stream, and achieve a higher level of economic security in their life. It's a great mom-and-pop business that you can run in your spare time while still working your 9:00 to 5:00 job. Hopefully, from reading the preceding chapters, you realize just how easy it is to get started in this business.

Of course, as you move ahead in your new business, you will find that there is plenty more to learn. We encourage you to read books, take classes, and talk to others in the business who may have been around the block a few more times than you.

## Jump right in

But, don't put pressure on yourself by thinking that you need to know everything there is to know about real estate investing before even taking the first step, or your ship will never leave the port. Instead, do like we did. Jump in and buy a property, and learn as you go along. Our experience has been that you learn a lot more by doing something, than by reading about it or watching others do it.

Take chances, make mistakes, and get messy!

Terry & Angy

# References

American Society of Home Inspectors
*http://www.ashi.org/*

*Blue Ribbon Home Warranty Survey Results.* 2012.
*www.blueribbonhomewarranty.com/inspect2.htm*

Brown, David, Ralph Warner, and Janet Portman. 2009.
*California Landlord's Law Book: Rights & Responsibilities.*
NOLO; 13th Edition.

Casler, Carlton. 2002. *Arizona Landlords' Deskbook,*
Consumer Law Books Publishing House; 4th edition.

Emerson, Ralph Waldo. *Self Reliance.*
*http://www.emersoncentral.com/selfreliance.htm*
Habitat for Humanity Stores.
http://www.habitat.org/restores/

Hess, Hermann. 2012. *Siddhartha.* Simon and Brown.

Homes for sale by the government.
*http://portal.hud.gov/hudportal/HUD?src=/topics/homes
_for_sale*

*NOLO. Law for All.*
*http://www.nolo.com/legal-encyclopedia/free-books/dog-
book/chapter4-7.html*

Stewart, Marsha, Ralph Warner, and Janet Portman. 2010.
*Every Landlord's Legal Guide.* NOLO 10th edition.
*www.Craigslist.org.* Run ads to rent your house.

*www.Eppraisal.com.* Internet appraisals.

*www.LendingTree.com.* Online mortgage information.

*www.MortgageLoan.com.* Online mortgage information.

*www.Zillow.com.* Information on house values and listings.

# Appendix

Turn Your Home Into a Rental House Instead of Selling It!

## Sample Month-to-Month Lease

(Disclaimer: This is just a sample agreement, it may not be appropriate for use in all states or under all circumstances.)

# Turn Your Home Into a Rental House Instead of Selling It!

Property: _____

Owner: YOUR NAME

_____

YOUR ADDRESS HERE
YOUR CITY, STATE, ZIP
YOUR PHONE

This rental agreement between

_____, known

herein as Lessors, and

_____,

known herein as Lessee(s), establishes the conditions by
which you may rent above described property which is a
_____ bedroom, _____bathroom house. This is a
month-to-month lease, beginning on
_____ and continuing indefinitely,
provided all terms and conditions of this agreement are
followed. Please read the following conditions so that you
will be fully apprised of your position as a renter of this
property.

1. All rents shall be paid promptly on or before the first
   day of each month, unless an exception is agreed upon
   in writing between the Lessors and Lessee(s) herewith
   _____. **Should the full rent
   payment be delinquent past the fifth day agreed
   upon, this rental agreement will have been
   violated** and the Lessee(s) are subject to vacate the
   premises upon notice, unless the Lessors, at their
   discretion, agree otherwise. If Lessee(s) are allowed to
   pay delinquent rents and remain on the premises, a late
   fee of 1% per day will be imposed on the amount that
   was late.

2.  Lessors may be entitled to immediate possession by instituting and maintaining statutory suit of forcible entry and detainer in the proper court, and writ of possession thereby.  Lessors may re-enter property by summary proceedings, or by force without being liable for prosecution therefore, and take possession of said premises and remove all persons and/or personal property. **This rent shall be due each month as agreed until either the Lessee(s) or the Lessors give written 30-day notification previous to the first day of the month of intent to terminate this agreement.**

3.  The Lessees shall respect the rights of neighbors to reasonable quiet.  NO loud parties are allowed. NO activity that violates any law, ordinance, rule, or regulation may occur on the premises, including illegal drugs, alcohol consumption, gambling, or prostitution.

4.  NO animals or pets are permitted on the premises unless expressly agreed to by the Lessors herewith _____. If pets are allowed, an additional monthly fee of $ _25 per month_ will be required for each pet.

5.  Personal property owned by the Lessee(s) shall not be left outside when not in use.  The Lessee(s) shall be responsible for all utilities consumed within the premises.  The Lessee(s) shall carry insurance on their personal belongings within the premises.

    The Lessee(s) shall keep all furnishings, appliances, fixtures, etc. functional, and in good, clean, undamaged condition.  They shall surrender the premises at the termination of the rental period in like condition as when taken. The Lessee(s) shall keep the entire property well maintained. The Lessee(s) shall be responsible for any damages to the premises or any furnishing, fixture, clogging of any sink, drain or other plumbing or mechanical function which is due to the Lessee(s)' neglect, abuse or misuse. They shall also be responsible for any glass breakage or damage to any of the Lessors' property caused by any act of the Lessee(s) or person/persons visiting the Lessee(s). The Lessee(s) shall contact the Lessors immediately regarding any plumbing, heating or lighting problems. The Lessee(s) agree(s) to maintain the property by proper and regular housekeeping procedures to the satisfaction of the Lessors. This includes but is not limited to maintaining the yard and shrubbery and watering same during dry weather. If Lessee(s) fail to maintain the premises as provided in this agreement, or cause damage to same, the Lessors shall have such repair or maintenance performed and the cost shall be added to the next rental payment due.

RENTAL RATE WILL BE INCREASED TO _____ IF YARDWORK IS NOT COMPLETED REGULARLY AND SATISFACTORILY.

6. The Lessors shall be entitled to enter upon the premises at all reasonable times to inspect, rent, offer for sale, or repair the premises regardless of whether the Lessee(s) may or may not be present. However, a reasonable effort (usually 48 hours) will be made to inform the Lessee(s) of an up-coming visit, if possible. Occupancy by others than the party or parties to whom the

property is specifically rented shall be in violation of this rental agreement.

The rental fee for this property is $_____ per month. The rental fee will be discounted to $_____ per month if the rent is RECEIVED by lessor on or before the due date. In the event the Lessors must travel to the property to collect any payments, an additional fee of $_____ will be assessed, however, the Lessors reserves the right to serve notice of eviction at such time. If an adjustment to this agreement needs to be made, a 30-day written notification will be given. The Lessee(s) understand that everyone so named is responsible to pay the rent jointly or individually. If Lessee(s) pay(s) rental fee by check and the check is returned for any reason, any discount will be rescinded and the above provisions will apply. The security deposit is $_____.

This deposit will be returned within 14 days of the end of the rental term provided that all rent is paid, all keys are returned, and all conditions of this rental agreement have been observed. The Lessors may apply all or any part of such deposit to the unpaid rent, damages, repair, or cleaning of the premises in the event the Lessee(s) fail to do so upon moving out.

7. The prospective Lessee(s) shall complete a rental application, grant permission to Lessors to check their credit, provide two letters of recommendation from present or former landlords, the security deposit AND

the first month's rent (or pro-rated rent) to the Lessors before the Lessee(s) occupy the premises.

8.  If rents become 10 or more days overdue and the lessees have been absent for 7 days, the property will be considered to be abandoned, and the Lessors shall have a lien upon all personal property found within the leased property (herein described), for all damage or amounts due and unpaid by Lessee(s), except property specifically exempt by law. Property shall be disposed of by Lessors as they see fit without recourse by Lessee(s). In the event we got to court, attorney fees, court costs, and other related fees will be awarded to the prevailing party.

9.  Lessors shall not be liable to Lessee(s) or to any other person for any damage to person(s) or property occasioned by any defects in said leased property, or by any other cause, or any act, omission, or neglect of Lessee(s) of said property, and Lessee(s) agree(s) to hold Lessors harmless from all claims from any such damages, whether the injury or loss occurs on or off said leased property. Lessee(s) should secure insurance to protect against the above occurrences. Lessee(s) agree(s) that existing locks and latches are safe and acceptable and no additional locks will be installed or changed without the consent of the Lessors.

10. No oral agreements have been made. This lease and option is the entire agreement between the parties, and it may be modified only in writing signed by all parties.

11. The rental application of the Lessee(s) is made part of this Lease Agreement. Any false or incorrect statement(s) or omission(s) on this application shall be a default, and the Lessors may immediately terminate this Lease Agreement.

12. The Lessors will give the Lessees their main telephone number (landline or cell) .

13. Tenant authorizes landlord to dispose of abandoned property left on the premises by tenant after tenancy has terminated, in any manner the landlord deems fit, where the landlord reasonably determines that the value of said property is so low that the cost of moving, storing, and conducting a public sale would exceed the amount that would be realized from the sale. Tenant holds landlord harmless for loss of property and/or value of said property disposed of under these circumstances.

14 Landlord and tenant agree that the prevailing party in any litigation, action, or controversy arising from this Rental Agreement shall be entitled to reimbursement of or, if appropriate, and award of reasonable attorney's fees, litigation, expenses and court costs incurred prior to trail, during trail, post-judgment and/or appeal, without regard to whether or not the matter is contested.

15. Tenants may not park more than one vehicle per Tenant on the Premises, and a total of two vehicles. Vehicles must be parked on the driveway. They may not be parked on the front yard. Commercial vehicles,

trailers and RV's shall not be parked on or near the Premises.

16. Maintenance and/or repair of vehicles are not permitted on the Premises, except for minor repairs to vehicles belonging to Tenant or Occupants. Minor repairs shall mean changing of tires or washing of vehicles. Tenants shall clean up any mess resulting from minor repairs.

17. A free copy of the Arizona Residential Landlord and Tenants Act is available from the Arizona Secretary of State's Office.

18. Air filters for the air conditioner and furnace must be changed monthly. Tenants will be liable for any damage caused to the air conditioner and furnace motor because filters were not changed.

19. Tenants will mail all rental checks to Landlords.

20. Tenants are responsible for paying all utilities.

21. No smoking is allowed inside of the rental property.

22. Waterbeds are not allowed to be used in the rental property.

The Lessee(s) shall acknowledge reading and receiving a copy of this rental agreement entered into this _____day of _____, 20_____by their endorsement below, and further agrees to abide by these provisions. It is agreed by all parties that move-in day will be _____, and move-out date will be will be the last day of the rental period.

Lessors:

_____

Owner/Manager Signature          Date

_____

Owner/Manager Signature          Date


Lessee(s):

_____

Tenant Signature          Date

_____

Tenant Signature          Date

# Tenant Application Form

# Turn Your Home Into a Rental House Instead of Selling It!

Date: _____

APPLICANT

Name:
_____

Present Address:
_____

How Long? _____

Previous Address:
_____

How Long? _____

Married: _____

Spouse's Name:
_____

Children? _____ How Many?
_____ Ages? _____

Pets? _____ What Kind?
_____ How Many? _____

YOUR EMPLOYMENT

Employer:
_____

Employer Address:
_____

Supervisor: _____ Bus.
Phone: _____

How Long on Present Job?
_____

 Annual Income: _____

SPOUSE'S EMPLOYMENT

Employer:

_____

 Employer Address:

_____

Supervisor: _____

Bus. Phone: _____

How Long on Present Job? _____

Annual Income: _____

REFERENCES

Bank:

_____

Phone: _____

Personal Reference:

_____

Phone: _____

Credit Reference:

_____

Phone: _____

Credit Reference:

_____

Phone: _____

Additional Information

Have you ever been convicted of a crime? Describe

_____

And Date of each one

_____

_____

Have you ever been evicted, declared bankruptcy or had a judgment? Describe and Date each one:

_____


_____


_____

I represent that the information provided in this application is true, complete and accurate to the best of my knowledge. I understand that any misrepresentation or omission of information is grounds for eviction.

I understand that the information provided might be used by Landlord to determine whether to accept this application. I authorize Landlord to verify all the information given in this application, including past rental information, personal references and employment information provided. I authorize the Landlord to obtain a current credit and criminal background check

I understand that this application is not a rental agreement and that this application does not create any obligation on the Landlord

Person to contact in case of emergency:
_____ Phone _____
Address

_____

The undersigned represent that the information provided in this application is true, complete, and accurate to the best of my knowledge. I understand that any misrepresentation or omission of information is grounds for eviction

Name _____

Signature _____

Date _____


Name _____

Signature _____

Date _____

# Tenant Selection Rating Sheet

# Turn Your Home Into a Rental House Instead of Selling It!

Minimum selection criteria:

-Must have verifiable monthly income of at least 3 times the rent
-Need credit score (FICO) over 600
-Provide copy of photo ID
-Must have no minimum convictions

A more advanced written criteria using the point system (you can modify the scoring system based on your personal priorities):

During interview & house showing:

1. Punctuality
	On time for appointment: 5 points
	Running late, called to inform: 3 points
	Late: 0-10 minutes: 2 points
	11-20 minutes: 0 points
	20+ minutes: landlord leaves, applicant rejected

2. Respectful and courteous: subjective, score -5 to 5
	To the landlord
	To each other
	Cursing, swearing, pushing, shoving, and violent behavior, demeaning speech or treatment of landlord or to one another: applicant rejected

3. Neat/clean appearance of all parties: 5 points

Application:

1. Attached copies of ID to application (Driver's license and social security card)
> Yes: 5 points
> No: 0 points

2. Filled out application entirely leaving no blanks
> Yes: 5 points
> No: -5 points, grounds for rejection

3. No errors on application form:
> Yes: 0 points – expected
> No: application rejected

4. Able to provide
> Verification of previous address: driver's license or utility bill: 5 points
> Proof of income, employment: pay stub: 5 points
> If self employed, a tax return or bank statement: 5 points

5. Able to pay first month's rent
> Yes: 0 points
> No: application rejected

6. Able to pay full amount of security deposit: 5 points
> Half of security deposit: 0 points

7. Monthly income = 3 times rent amount (if rent is $1,000, they make $3,000/month)
> Higher; 3x-4x: 5 points
> 3x: 0 points

2x or below; application is rejected

8. Stable income or employment
For 3+ years: 5 points
1-3 years: 3 points
0-1 year: 0 points

9. Credit history (FICO score)
Over 700: 10 points
650-700: 5 points
600-650: 2 points
Below 600: 0 points
Bankruptcy: -10 points

10. At current address for a minimum of:
1 year: 3 points
1+ years: 5 points
Less than 1 year: -5 points

11. None, or small, pets: 5 points
Vicious dogs, snakes, reptiles, or large birds:
application rejected

12.Non-smoker: 10 points

Background Check/Screening:

Name must not appear on Sex Offenders Registry.

Criminal history may not contain drug offenses within 7 years.

Criminal history must not contain felony convictions within 7 years for violent crimes or property crimes.

Score _____

Applicant: Accepted _____   Rejected _____

# Property Inspection Sheet

# Turn Your Home Into a Rental House Instead of Selling It!

.

# Property Inspection Sheet
## (Move in /Move Out)

Property address:
_____

*This form is for the protection of both our residents and the owners. It protects tenants from being charged for any pre-existing damage or wear to the property. The form protects the owners against any shortage of fixtures or appliances, damage to property, unusual wear to the property caused by the tenant. Cost of repairs will be charged to the tenant's security deposit.*

**Number of keys given to tenant:**

Date:

|  | MOVE IN | MOVE OUT | CHARGES |
|---|---|---|---|
| KITCHEN **cabinets condition** | | | |
| cabinets clean | | | |
| REFRIGERATOR **clean?** | | | |
| 2 ice cube trays | | | |
| 2 shelves & 2 vegetable drawers | | | |
| light bulb | | | |
| ice caddie | | | |
| STOVE **clean & working?** | | | |
| oven racks clean | | | |
| Oven walls clean | | | |
| light bulb | | | |
| DISPOSAL **clean & working?** | | | |

# Turn Your Home Into a Rental House Instead of Selling It!

| | | | |
|---|---|---|---|
| COUNTER TOP condition | | | |
| FAN, FILTER, HOOD clean? | | | |
| BATHROOM #1 clean? | | | |
| SOAP DISHES, towel bars | | | |
| shower rod, toilet paper holder | | | |
| faucets & drains work properly | | | |
| caulking & tile clean | | | |
| fan clean/working | | | |
| BATHROOM #2 clean? | | | |
| SOAP DISHES, towel bars | | | |
| shower rod, toilet paper holder | | | |
| faucets & drains work properly | | | |
| caulking & tile clean | | | |
| fan clean & working | | | |
| HEATING AND AIR COND. | | | |
| clean & working | | | |
| furnace filters | | | |
| DOORS work properly? | | | |
| door knobs work | | | |
| door locks work | | | |
| WINDOWS work properly? | | | |
| windows clean | | | |

| | | | |
|---|---|---|---|
| screens | | | |
| security windows | | | |
| BROKEN/CRACKED windows? | | | |
| CONDITION of doors, frames | | | |
| condition of woodwork | | | |
| CARPETS clean yes or no? | | | |
| burns, tears ,stains (name) | | | |
| CURTAIN RODS & fixtures | | | |
| BLINDS & shades | | | |
| RUBBISH removed? | | | |
| LIGHTING fixtures & bulbs | | | |
| WALLS surfaces clean | | | |
| not repainted or wallpapered by tenant | | | |
| VENTS & registers work? | | | |
| ELECTRICAL outlets work? | | | |
| cover plates on outlets | | | |
| MIRRORS clean? | | | |
| SMOKE detectors work? | | | |

## COMMENTS:

By signing our name below I/we (tenants) accept the Property Inspection Sheet as a part of the rental agreement and agree that it is an accurate account of the condition and contents of the premises and acknowledge receiving a copy hereof. I/we (tenants) also agree to pay for any damages to the property and contents other than normal wear.

TENANT_____ DATE_____

TENANT_____ DATE_____


MANAGER/OWNER _____ DATE_____

MANAGER/OWNER _____ DATE_____

# Move In Information Sheet for Tenants

# Turn Your Home Into a Rental House Instead of Selling It!

## Move In Information Sheet:
## Helpful Information and Reminders for Tenants
## 2551 N. Banyon Street

1. Put electrical and water service in your name by Wednesday.

2. Change filter in air conditioner/furnace monthly.

3. Furnace doesn't work when outside temperature is below 32 degrees. Use electrical heaters when this happens.

4. If dish washer doesn't work, turn screw below washer with fingers.

5. Use only paper logs or small wooden logs in fire place.

6. Trash and recycle pickup is Monday; place barrels next to the street for pickup.

7. The electrical switch box is located on the outside of the garage next to the sidewalk.

8. The emergency water shut-off valve is located below the bay windows in the front of the house.

Mail rental checks to:

PO Box 3333
Tucson, AZ 85799
By the 1st of each month

Call Terry or Angy at 270-xxxx with any questions or problems.

Turn Your Home Into a Rental House Instead of Selling It!

# Tenant Move Out Information Letter

# Turn Your Home Into a Rental House Instead of Selling It!

October 23, 20xx
Jenny xxxx
xxxx S. Avenida Sirio

Dear Jenny,

You stated that you will move out November 30, 20xx . If you move out sooner, we will pro-rate your monthly payment so that you only pay for the days that you are actually in the house.

We wish you good luck in the future. We have enjoyed a good working relationship with you, and we want your move out to go smoothly.

Moving time can be frenzied and you have many things on your mind, including getting the maximum amount of your security deposit back. We want to be able to return your security deposit promptly and in full. Your security deposit is $800, $150 of which non-refundable and used for house sanitation (an ozone treatment of the entire house).

We expect your rental house to be in the same condition it was when you moved in. Of course, some wear and tear is normal and acceptable. A copy of your signed Property Inspection Checklist is attached in case your copy is not handy. We will use this checklist when we inspect the rental house upon your moving-out and will deduct the cost for required cleaning and repairs that we observe, beyond what could be considered ordinary wear and tear, from your security deposit.

In order to receive a full refund, make sure that all items are clean and free from damage, except for ordinary wear and tear. All closets, cabinets, shelves, drawers, countertops, storage, refrigerator and exterior areas should be completely free of items. Please be sure to remove all personal possessions, including furniture, clothes, household items, food, plants, cleaning supplies, and any bags of garbage or loose items that belong to you.

Please contact your phone, cable, and utility providers and schedule the disconnection of services in your name. Also, cancel magazine and newspaper subscriptions, and submit a change of address to the U.S. Postal Service.

To arrange an inspection of your rental unit, please contact us when all the conditions above have been satisfied. You will be charged a key replacement fee if you do not return all keys at the time of the inspection. Leave a forwarding address if you wish your security deposit mailed to you.

We will return the security deposit to you either in person or at the address provided within 10 days after you move out and return all keys. If you have any overdue rent or other unpaid charges, or damages to the property, or you fail to properly clean, we will include an explanation of the charges along with the balance of your security deposit.

If you have any questions, contact us at 270-xxxx.

Sincerely,

XXXXX

Owners/Managers

# Sample Letter for Tenant to do Yard Work

MEMO
Date: November 5, 20xx
To: xxxx and xxxx
Location: 2551 N. Banyon Blvd.
Re: Yard work

This is just a friendly reminder that the front yard looks like might need a little maintenance. We noticed that the weeds were starting to take over the yard a little.

If you could tidy it up a bit, we'd appreciate it. If you need a weed wacker just let us know. We'd be happy to loan you one.

We are very grateful to have you as tenants. You have been really great about taking caring of the property.

If anything comes up where you need any help with repairs, or anything else, please don't hesitate to contact us.

(If you have already done this yard clean up, please disregard this letter.)

With best regards,
Terry & Angy Sprouse
270-xxxx

Turn Your Home Into a Rental House Instead of Selling It!

# Index

## About the Authors

Terry and Angy Sprouse have been involved in real estate since 2001. They live in Tucson., Arizona with their two sons, and with Blackie the Wonder Dog & Tabby the egotistical cat.

In their spare time, they like to take the dog walking, spoil the cat, and attempt to keep up with their sons' nonstop teen-related activities.

Their wish for the future is that the cat will stop stepping on their heads while they are trying to sleep.

For more information about real estate investing and book publishing, visit Terry's blog at:

*www.fixemuprentemout.com*

134